Built to Last
A Showcase of Concrete Homes

ina Skinner

Schiffer Publishing Ltd

4880 Lower Valley Road, Atglen, PA 19310 USA

Photo credits
Front cover: *Courtesy of Portland Cement Association*
Back cover: *Courtesy of Harrison Design Associates* and © *Rob Mair*
Page 1, 2 & 3: *Courtesy of Curt Hofer Construction, Inc.*

Library of Congress Cataloging-in-Publication Data

Skinner, Tina.
Built to last : a showcase of concrete homes / Tina Skinner.
p. cm.
ISBN 0-7643-1617-6
1. Architecture, Domestic--United States--20th century. 2. Concrete houses--
United States. I. Title.
NA7208 .S58 2002
728'.37'0973--dc21
2002001589

Designed by Bonnie M. Hensley
Cover design by Bruce M. Waters
Type set in Zurich LtCn BT/Zurich BT

ISBN: 0-7643-1617-6
Printed in China

Published by Schiffer Publishing Ltd.
4880 Lower Valley Road
Atglen, PA 19310
Phone: (610) 593-1777; Fax: (610) 593-2002
E-mail: Schifferbk@aol.com
Please visit our web site catalog at **www.schifferbooks.com**
We are always looking for people to write books on new and related subjects. If
you have an idea for a book, please contact us at the above address.

This book may be purchased from the publisher.
Include $3.95 for shipping. Please try your bookstore first.
You may write for a free catalog.

In Europe, Schiffer books are distributed by
Bushwood Books
6 Marksbury Ave. Kew Gardens
Surrey TW9 4JF England
Phone: 44 (0)20 8392-8585; Fax: 44 (0)20 8392-9876
E-mail: Bushwd@aol.com
Free postage in the UK. Europe: air mail at cost.
Please try your bookstore first.

Contents

Acknowledgements

The talented team at the Portland Cement Association (PCA) is paid to promote the use of concrete, though that doesn't taint their passion for the subject. They helped me spell out the obvious advantages, as well as the extra bonuses that come with spending a few dollars more per square foot of home. Besides hoping to spell out the reasons why we should be building any permanent structure with concrete, the PCA folks are equally excited about the little projects. Much of the vision and the effort for this book originated with PCA staff members Jennifer Grover and Jim Niehoff. They brought together their extensive network of friends and associates to create this wonderful collection of award winning and showplace homes. Besides their efficiency and effectiveness, it is hard to find two people more pleasant to work with.

Additionally, research on this book has led me to architects, designers, contractors, and homeowners equally enthralled with concrete houses. Their excitement is accurately reflected in these gorgeous homes. Enjoy!

Introduction

"The Rock" earned its nickname for its solid concrete walls within a European-style, castle-like facade. *Courtesy of Bost Construction Company*

What is an ICF System?

They say beauty is only skin deep, and it couldn't be more true in the case of a home. Wood, brick, stone, or aluminum siding can conceal any number of problems in a home's construction. Or benefits.

Imagine your home's frame as the skeleton or bones of the house. Today's standard, wood-frame home gives you a series of 2x4s spaced wide enough to walk through. On the outside, some form of foam insulation is tacked on to improve the R-value or insulation of the home, and then covered in your selected siding. Inside you have wallboard. An intruder could bash his way in with a hammer, or simply cut through with a knife.

Cramer Gallimore Photography Studio, Raleigh, NC

In the case of *insulating concrete form* (ICF) construction, you get a steel-reinforced, solid concrete set of bones, with a warm wrapping of foam insulation. Then you add whatever beautiful skin you like.

Energy efficient, element resistant – the safety, economic, and environmental advantages of building with concrete add up with every square foot you pour. A simple system, relatively new to North America, makes it possible for construction crews to rapidly set up manufactured foam forms and pour concrete walls quickly and efficiently.

Traditionally, cast-in-place concrete homes require temporary molds to be built

Don't let appearances fool you. This solid concrete home was made rustic with cedar siding and shakes, native stone veneer, and an exposed log roof structure. *Courtesy of Ed Zweigle Enterprises*

©Zweigle-Ratiner Studios, Truckee, CA

of plywood, steel, or aluminum. After placing steel bars to reinforce the wall, the crew pours concrete inside the cavity. Once the concrete hardens, the crew strips the forms to leave the reinforced concrete walls.

With ICF construction, the foam mold is left in place. It helps cure the concrete, and then acts as insulation for the home, and a convenient surface for inserting plumbing and wiring, and attaching wallboard, stucco, and other decorative treatments.

ICF technology has been used by European builders for more than three decades. Concrete home building is standard in most areas of Europe. Though it has been available for commercial and residential construction in the United States since 1978, ICF construction didn't really begin to catch on until the 1990s. ICFs are now in new homes across every region and in every price range.

ICFs are produced with expanded or extruded polystyrene, often using up to 20 percent recycled materials. Steel reinforcing bars are placed vertically and horizontally within the form, and the cavity is then filled with concrete. Unlike plywood, steel, or aluminum molds, ICFs are left in place after the concrete hardens. These foam forms provide two inches of insulation on both faces of a concrete wall, which is usually about six inches thick depending on the manufacturer.

Two basic types of ICF systems are available. One uses hollow, polystyrene blocks that stack and interlock, almost like children's building blocks. The other uses panels or planks that are held a constant distance apart by a series of plastic ties. Both result in an end-product wall that is solid, strong, and super energy efficient. The 10-inch (25cm) assembly with permanent insulation allows builders to create walls that rate from R-20 to R-56 – up to three times that of a conventional house.

A contemporary home defies description while defining elegance. *Courtesy of Precision Concrete Construction, Inc.*

Texas ranch-style home would look at home on the plains. *Courtesy of Portland Cement Association*

A new Southern Plantation. *Courtesy of A&S Steel Framing, Inc.*

A flared stairway provides an inviting entry to this elegantly symmetrical home. *Courtesy of A&S Steel Framing, Inc.*

1856—Famed journalist and travel guide Horace Greeley built the first U.S. concrete home on record at his Chappaqua, New York, estate.

1908—To fulfill his utopian dream of affordable, durable housing, inventor Thomas Edison builds eleven houses in New Jersey with his patented system for concrete homes. The homes still stand today.

1937—Frank Lloyd Wright casts his home-design masterpiece—Fallingwater—in concrete. "The first house in my experience built of reinforced concrete—the form took the grammar of that construction."

1971—First U.S. patent issued for insulating concrete forms.

Early 1980s—Insulating concrete forming systems now offered commercially in the U.S.

1985—Insulating concrete forms first introduced at The Builders' Show.

1993—Skyrocketing and volatile timber prices rekindle interest in alternatives to lumber such as concrete and steel.

1994—National Association of Home Builders builds its new technology showcase project, the New American Home, with concrete walls.

1994—Insulating concrete forms first show up on the statistical radar screen, with more than 1,000 concrete homes (0.1 percent of all housing starts). Conventional concrete block systems climb to 3.5 percent of the housing market or 38,000 homes.

1995—*Hometime*, a popular PBS home improvement show, airs a twelve-part series covering construction of an ICF home.

1995—U.S. Department of Housing and Urban Development cites concrete as a leading alternative to lumber in its landmark report, *Innovative Structural Systems for Home Construction*

1996—More than 6,000 homes are built with insulating concrete forms—a six-fold increase from 1994. More than 57,000 block homes are built, accounting for 5.5 percent of all housing starts.

1996—Aerated concrete, a block-like product well established in European and Japanese housing, makes its U.S. debut with a factory in Atlanta, Georgia. More than 1,000 aerated concrete homes are built that year.

1997—ICF's thermal mass and energy-savings recognized in National Energy Code

1997—Study by Boston University Professor Pieter VanderWerf finds that concrete homes consume 32 to 44 percent less energy for heating and cooling than wood-frame homes.

1997—ICFs featured in *Better Homes &Garden's* Architect's Best Small House

1999—Concrete homes are projected to reach 13.1 percent of all housing starts by the end of the year: 35,500 ICF homes, 88,100 block homes, and 5,100 aerated concrete homes.

2001—Concrete homes command 15 percent of market share in the United States, and climbing.

Why Would You Want Concrete?

Your wallet is probably the first sensible consideration when deciding what kind of home you want to live in. Though ICF construction may add 5-10 percent to a new home's cost, there are economic advantages that should be taken into consideration. As far as your investment is concerned, a concrete home is more durable, with three times the life expectancy of a wood-frame home. This durability increases the home's desirability and value when resale time comes around.

While you're living in the home, there are energy cost savings to consider. Concrete saves energy by its sheer mass – concrete slows the passage of heat moving through the wall. A concrete wall has fewer air leaks than wood-frame walls, and air leakage accounts for a large percentage of the energy loss in a home. That, plus the built-in foam insulation mean that an ICF-system home stays warmer in the winter and cooler in the summer than a wood-frame home.

Because outer walls are more energy efficient, homes can be built with smaller heating and air conditioning systems – an initial savings in purchase price for the home. Over the long run, research indicates that concrete homeowners can save an average of 44 per-cent on their heating costs, 32 per-cent on cooling.

You may save money on insurance, too. Insurance companies recognize the safety features of concrete homes, and your rate should reflect that fact. ICF walls can withstand up to four hours of intense fire and temperatures without structural failure. And they can resist debris driven by 250 mph tornado-force winds. Moreover, calculations show that steel-reinforced concrete walls may have more than twice the bending capacity of a wood frame wall.

On a more practical level, nature has more subtle challenges your home will be likely to face than the dramatic threats of fire and storm. Termites, carpenter ants, and other wood-boring insects can cause severe structural damage to a wood-frame home. And there's dry rot, too, a common timber disease caused by fungi.

There are bigger pests to consider, as well. Most frame-built homes can be broken into with a pocketknife. That's all it takes to cut between the 2x4 studs, slicing through the paper, foam, and plastic wall systems. ICF homes offer up to six inches of solid steel and concrete in your wall. Enough to deflect most bullets. So you're buying solid peace of mind with solid concrete construction.

There are invisible advantages, too. The same solid construction that keeps heating and cooling bills down also keeps out pollens and other environmental aggravations. ICF walls allow only about one half the air penetration as conventional homes, so fewer dust particles and other contaminants pass through the walls. The inert building materials may be better for your health, too. Studies have found that volatile organic compound emissions from concrete building products are lower than those observed for most other building materials and do not present a health risk.

For your ears, approximately one-third as much sound gets through an ICF wall compared to an ordinary frame wall. You'll be less likely to be awakened by the neighbor's lawn mower, a passing motorcycle, or a teenager's super bass sound system. As land becomes more expen-

Zalewa Image Designers, Georgetown, IN

sive, and building lots shrink, these invisible sound barriers will be important assets in neighborhood peacekeeping efforts. As for your eyes, once the home is complete, you can't tell the difference between concrete and wood frame.

"We wanted to build a home that would be our last home," say proud owners Dr. Bruce and Coby Watier of Indiana. "Another important factor was our preference to the stucco or Dryvit exterior efface. Due to concerns regarding stucco and the rotting effects using traditional wood framing, we needed another option. The only option was ICF." *Courtesy of The Watier Family and Essroc, Inc.*

Named the New American Home, this project, sponsored by the National Association of Home Builders incorporates ICF technology for both interior and exterior walls, plus cutting-edge colors and textures for the concrete flatwork. The home is environmentally friendly, fireproof, energy efficient, and beautiful. Because concrete walls were used for the interior, fewer interior walls were needed. Moreover, concrete's sound-deadening qualities are an important contribution to these wonderful, open spaces. *Courtesy of Portland Cement Association*

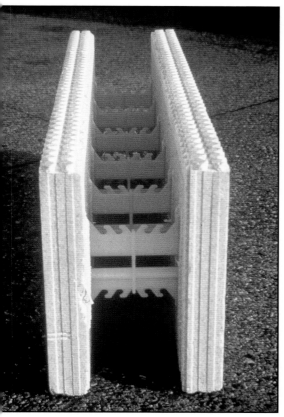

Close-up view of an interlocking insulated concrete form (ICF).

Building with Concrete

If you're eager to move into your new home, ICF construction may speed the process. Choose a contractor experienced with concrete wall systems and construction can take a fraction of the time required with wood or steel frame. You get a higher quality of wall, and less-skilled laborers can be employed, according to Jim Smart, a partner in Lake Crest Homes. His company selected ICF construction for an entire neighborhood of homes in a country club community in Nevada. The initial cutting and placement of the ICF forms requires exactitude, but once in place, any novice could undertake the insertion of steel reinforcing rods and pouring the cement, Smart said.

Although it looks new and different, anyone with construction experience can quickly get up to speed with ICFs. An ideal crew has a mix of concrete placement and carpentry experience. Once the crew has some practice, each ICF-built home requires less skilled labor and less total

Weighing about five pounds each, ICFs are easily lifted and stacked.

labor than a wood-framed home, according to the Portland Cement Association. Actually, ICF construction has big advantages for the workers. the foam is light and power equipment moves the concrete. So crews stay fresh and sharp. In fact, the simplicity of assembly and the lightness of the work help keep labor costs below those of frame construction.

The insulation provided by the forms also gives builders the ability to successfully place concrete even during extremes of weather. Few weather conditions affect a pour because the form insulates the concrete, allowing it to cure almost regardless of outside temperature or humidity. During construction, the forms function like thermos bottles: the insulation forces the water to leave the concrete at a lower rate diminishing the risk of serious cracks.

Steel rebar is placed both vertically and horizontally within the cavity as the forms are stacked.

Foam ICFs are quickly altered to fit varying architectural needs. Here an ordinary handsaw is put to use to cut an ICF.

A "window buck" is placed to preserve a future view after the concrete is poured.

Stacked and braced walls are ready for pumping. Because the forms come with their own insulation, this snow is not going to delay the pour.

Likewise, ICFs present no problem for the sub-contractors who come after the walls are poured. Since holes, chases, and rectangles are easily cut into ICFs with a knife or saw, installation of mechanical systems is a snap. Electricians cut channels for cables and wires into the forms. Plumbers work in a similar way, placing cold and hot water lines in the insulation after the concrete is poured. The new walls are compatible with regular windows and doors, too. The fastening of drywall and lap siding is just as fast and easy. And midcourse corrections, such as moving an opening, are no big deal – just saw it out and re-form. It's not more difficult to make changes to an ICF wall, it's just different.

Unlike wood, a home built out of concrete dramatically reduces the chance of shrinkage, twisting, rotting and settlement," says Frank Brock, whose company Brock & Weigl distributes the ARXX ICF system.

"Wood is getting more and more expensive and the quality is going down," says Clifford Taylor, an architect based in Colorado Springs. Besides cost and initial quality, wood presents challenges in construction and the longevity of the home. "Wood is constantly warping," he said. "We work almost exclusively in concrete."

Historically, concrete prices have been remarkably stable. So price increases in other materials have helped to generate interest in concrete building systems. Concrete is becoming one of the most cost competitive walls systems in the North American housing markets.

Certainly, building in concrete has business advantages for the contractor. Gary Schwartz, who built a showcase home in St. Louis, enjoyed surprising people during thirteen-days of tours with the fact that the "wood" siding on his home was actually concrete product with a 50-year guarantee; that his ICF walls were virtually indestructible and soundproof, and that the cultured stone around a beautiful fireplace was, you guessed it, concrete. "Most people had no idea," Schwartz said. Because his concrete show home was written about in local publications as a standout attraction in a development full of showcase homes, "many people came just to see this house."

Schwartz continues to hear from people ready to build a home, and ready to build it of concrete. "Once consumers hear about it and see it, they come looking for you," he said. "We're building three houses right now, and one is almost identical to the showcase home. People really liked this home. They all want copies. The first year we built an ICF house we built three or four. The next year we built ten to twelve. Next year we expect to build twenty." He's also expanding his firm to include a branch that cuts and places ICFs for other builders who want to provide concrete homes to their customers.

The concrete mixers arrive and pumping begins.

15

It's not just a matter of educating homebuyers, says Monica M. Muro, who does marketing for A&S Steel Framing and Arxx High Performance Wallsystem. "Everyone that's coming to us is already sold on ICF," she said. These days consumers are educating themselves, Muro said. They're going online and getting lots of information on the internet. By the time they contact a designer or builder, they've often made up their minds about what they want. The problem they may encounter is that the builder, or the architect, even engineers, may not know anything about ICF construction, and they may dissuade homeowners from using this kind of building system.

So Muro runs a series of continuing education courses for professionals – architects and engineers, inspectors and building officials, real estate agents, and contractors and builders — to bring them up to date on the ICF construction. Armed with the facts, these people also become powerful advocates for her company's concrete homes.

"We built two in 1997, and we're doing about 52 homes this year. Churches, too – we're on our fifth church now. That comes through building a home for someone in the congregation – they understand the advantages," Muro said.

Her Florida customers have regional reasons for wanting the best that ICF has to offer. For one, there's the energy savings on cooling costs. Primarily, though, there's the safety factor. "We work with FEMA (Federal Emergency Management Agency). Their motto is run from the wind, hide from the water. So if you can stay home, that's better. Our waterfront homeowners are leaving home (in the case of hurricanes), but they're coming back to a house that's still standing."

With these considerations in mind, Muro said the two to five percent in additional building costs have not deterred her customers. "Not one!"

The top of the forms are "troweled off" after the pumping.

A house with completed concrete walls is ready to be roofed and drywalled.

Channels are cut in the interior foam insulation to run electrical wire and plumbing. The cuts can be made using a hand-held knife.

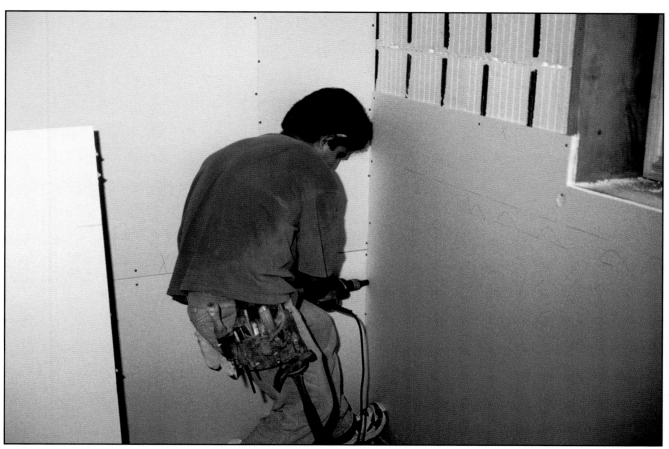

Drywall is attached to the interior surface of the foam and concrete wall using screws.

Any standard exterior application can be applied. Here masons apply brick fascia.

One Contractor's Experience

Specializing in ICF construction gives luxury home contractors a decided edge in the new homes marketplace. That's been the experience of Ontario homebuilder Ed Loyens and his sons, Mike and Travis. Ed Loyens built his first ICF home 23 years ago, when he owned a ready mix concrete company and did a pour for another contractor. Today there are still many architects and contractors who have never used, or even heard of, ICF wall systems. But Loyens remembered. Years later, with his own contracting company, Riverstone Design and Build, he returned to the process.

The Loyens family made their mark when they signed up to build a showcase home in London, Ontario, with the Cement Association of Canada.

"We got involved because we wanted to build higher quality homes. Also, we felt that the move to ICF construction would give us a competitive advantage over companies doing frame construction," Ed Loyens said. As a result of his ICF-built show home in Ontario, Loyens is taking orders for new concrete homes. His hypothesis that people would pay a little extra for the comfort and safety of concrete walls has proven dead on accurate.

"It costs about eight percent more, but you get 100 percent more value in terms of comfort in the house," Loyens said. "We feel the customer is absolutely getting more value. It truly, truly is second to none as far as quality goes."

"ICF is simply a better product, especially for the type of customer we serve. There are a lot of Europeans in this area, and they are an easy sell with ICF and radiant heating because it's more familiar to them," says Travis Loyens. "And the farmers and rural people in this area also appreciate how solid and draft-free ICF construction is."

In general, Ed Loyens points out, a new $500,000 home gets the exact same quality of construction with stick-built or wood frame as an $80,000 home. People who investigate a little further when building or buying a luxury home discover the advantages in air and sound quality, plus energy savings, and longevity. "These houses will last 200 years," Loyens says proudly. "These aren't houses that are going to shrink or settle here and there."

The learning curve is fairly simple when making the switch from building wood frame to ICF construction. "It's pretty basic," Ed Loyens said. "I wouldn't recommend that someone who has no knowledge of

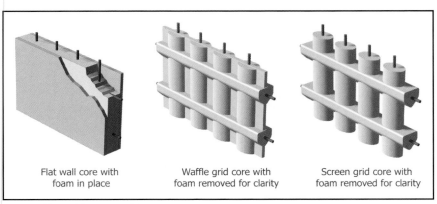

Flat wall core with foam in place

Waffle grid core with foam removed for clarity

Screen grid core with foam removed for clarity

Courtesy of Portland Cement Association

Before and after shots of the Loyens' family project, building a home to showcase the advantages of ICF construction. *Courtesy of Riverstone Design and Build*

construction try it. We understand concrete, because we owned a concrete business. You also have to understand forming and framing. You need braces and scaffolding, and if you follow the rules, it works quite nicely."

It's been a boon to his business. "There's an advantage to be doing something no one else does," he adds, "to specialize in an item. I think you'll end up building fewer homes, but of higher quality in a higher price range."

"It's definitely the way of the future," he concludes.

Getting Started

If you have decided that a concrete home is the way to go for your comfort and peace of mind, you'll still face lots of options. For one thing, there are many ways to build a concrete home, including concrete masonry or block construction, cast-in-place walls, and the relatively new autoclaved aerated concrete blocks that are lightweight and easy to cut using hand tools. The Portland Cement Association can provide technical data on all forms of concrete construction: phone 847-966-6200 or visit www.concretehomes.com.

If you've decided that ICF construction is the best route for your new home, the companies that make ICFs provide extensive information, including the names of experienced contractors in their area. Builders can get product specifications, instructions, and training. A good start might be the Insulating Concrete Form Association; phone 847-657-9730 or visit www.forms.org.

Tour of Homes

On the following pages, you are invited to tour fifteen outstanding showcase homes. These homes were built for a variety of reasons, whether to raise money for charitable causes, or simply to raise awareness of ICF construction among contractors, architects, developers, and, most importantly, the home-buying public.

Each of these homes is so unique, so different from the others. This is an excellent opportunity to try to narrow down your own tastes in architectural styles and interior design. Together these homes illustrate how flexible concrete wall systems can be, adapting to any style of home design.

Many people paid for their tours, and they had to travel to get there. You are invited to kick back in a comfortable chair and let your fingers, so to speak, do the walking!

1. Crescent Nest

One of the wonderful things about constructing with concrete is the amazing design flexibility. Here is a home that embodies concrete's ability to fill the most dramatic of design ideas – a home that eschews straight walls.

Carte Blanc from the customers came with just a couple of tiny, but very daunting, criteria for architect Clifford Taylor of Colorado Springs. The homeowners wanted no straight walls, no parallel walls, and complete privacy with lots of open light and doors to the outside.

Returning to their home state after life on a sailboat in the Caribbean, Roger Loo and his wife, Destiny, were anything but your average square-box dwellers.

The nautilus-shaped home that they inspired won the American Concrete Institute's Award of Excellence. Less than 3,000-square feet in size, it makes a huge lifestyle statement in a wooded valley of red sandstone monoliths 15 miles south of Colorado Springs, embracing a wooded hillside.

Clifford Taylor Architects planned the home as a series of pure radii in response to the owner's request that the use of right angles and parallel straight walls be minimized. The inner side of the curve is primarily glass where one can gaze out onto private terraces, views, and forest to the west. A pavilion is planned at the apex of that view. The enclosing mass – the exterior wall at the back of the house is almost solid concrete — protects the outdoor living areas from nearby noises, and encloses this private retreat.

At the center of the house is a seven-foot square, 22-foot high tower serving both as a dramatic entry and a chimney for passive natural ventilation.

The most unique feature of this home is the privacy, yet openness it provides us," say the

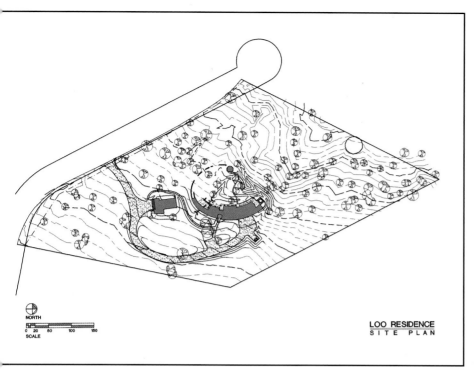

LOO RESIDENCE
SITE PLAN

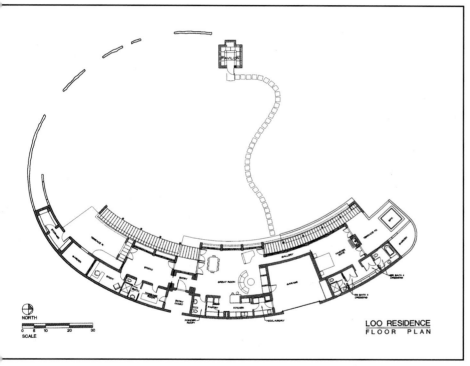

LOO RESIDENCE
FLOOR PLAN

A site plan shows how this crescent-shaped home was nestled into a hillside, amidst existing trees. Extension of the outer wall to continue the seashell shape, and a pavilion are planned for later construction.

owners. Besides the nearby highway, Loo adds that nearby Fort Carson serenades his neighbors with frequent bomb explosions. He hears none of it. "We have kind of a sanctuary on the inside of the house," he marvels. "We got everything we asked for – absolute privacy with complete openness, two opposite things."

"The design works remarkably well. It is absolutely quiet in the house. The convex wall bounces noise away and dispels it," remarked Clifford Taylor.

"The unique thing about this house is that all the interior walls are also ICF concrete," says Chuck Lipari of EPS Building Systems L.L.C. "This makes the house very quiet, nearly soundproof room to room. The homeowners gave the architect tremendous freedom in the design, and he is a big advocate of concrete walls. It was quite a project, especially with the curved walls. Quite a challenge," Lipari reminisces. "We were able to modify the shape of the forms, so no wood was wasted."

The first step was modifying the 9-1/4-inch ICF eForms by Reward Wall System, Lipari explains. Cuts were made on the outer side of the foam form – in this case these varied from 1/8-inch to 1/4-inch within each block of a four-foot long waffle grid ICF. The foam form was then bowed and temporarily anchored in its curved shape while the concrete was poured. The Masonite anchors were then removed and the inner walls were finished with drywall. The exterior walls were finished in genuine concrete stucco.

Slab concrete on grade was installed with radiant heat, adding to the comfort and energy efficiency of the home.

The inside curve of the semi-circular home is essentially glass, facing a private courtyard and mountain view. "My wife has a thing for doors. We have 11 doors going to the outside," says owner Roger Loo.

Opposite page: Matching wood floori and ceiling give this living room its uniq character. A wood beam works as crov molding, tying in with the contempora Arts and Crafts theme of the hon

Photography by Gaylon Wampler Studios

An exterior wall provides privacy and soundproofing against a nearby highway. At the center of the house is a seven-foot square, 22-foot high tower serving both as a dramatic entry and a chimney for passive natural ventilation.

Photography by Gaylon Wampler Studios

Photography by Gaylon Wampler Studios

A curved gallery wall connects living area with the whimsical master bedroom, where fluffy white bedding and butterfly pillows allow one to dream of floating amidst the clouds. Inspired by a life on Caribbean waters, Destiny Loo picked an interior color palette unique in this region of the Colorado Rockies.

2. Country Club Cottage

Built within an exclusive, country club community, the Cottages at Montreux live up to their name. The French-style architectural details in the home's construction include a tile roof with copper gutters and roof flashings, hardwood floors, slab granite countertops, hand-forged wrought iron railings, and paneled wood doors. A seamless lifestyle between indoors and out is created using an inner courtyard surrounded by porches, balconies, shutters, and turrets.

In choosing a construction style for this 3,747 square-foot home, an insulating concrete form by ARXX, distributed by Brock & Weigl, was chosen. Despite an increase in cost over steel or wood, concrete seemed a natural in this Nevada community, the builders agreed. The region's dry climate takes a toll on traditional lumber built homes. The arid, blustery elements tend to dehydrate wood, causing it to shrivel, twist, and contort. Fire is also a risk.

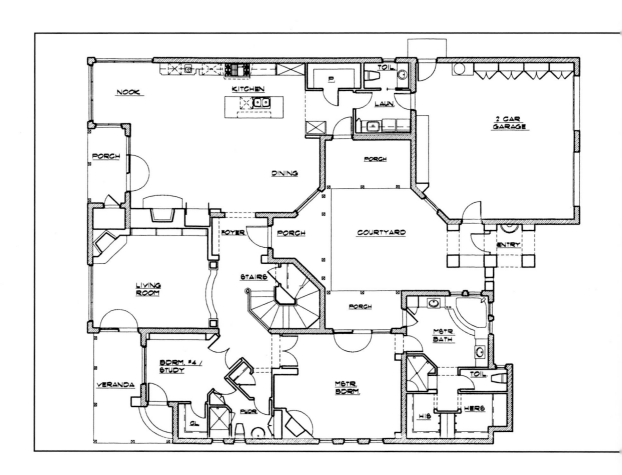

Energy efficiency was another consideration because of the fluctuating climes of the Silver State. Builder Jim Smrt, a partner in Lake Crest Homes, describes the concrete structure as an important element of what was planned as a luxury home. "With the right product type, people will be willing to pay for them, especially since they offer so many benefits over other traditional materials," he said.

"One of the most important benefits," says Frank Brock, of Brock & Weigle, is the protection factor. "A home is one of the biggest investments that people make in their lifetime. It makes sense to protect that investment," he said, adding that ICF construction adds an average seven percent to the home's cost.

"We just believe in this type of building; it makes more sense. Institutions like post offices and other government buildings have to be built for strength. The ICF technology brings that kind of thinking into the residential market. A house should be able to last two to three times longer when it's built that way. We see a lot of room for growth in this area."

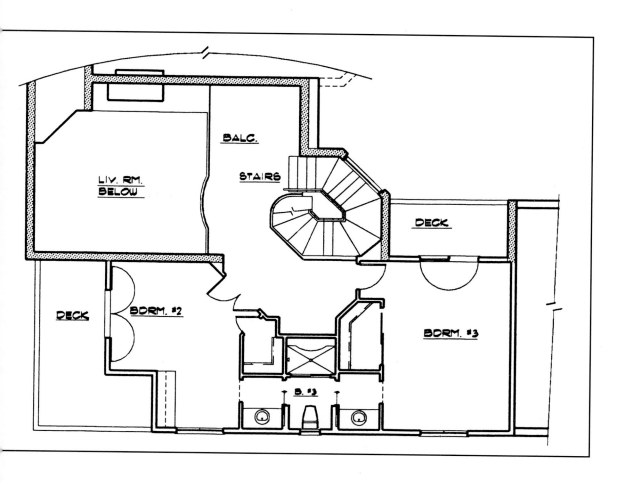

...chie and Associates Architects strove to create a home that looked as though it had been in place for ...hundred years when they designed this charming yet spacious French country cottage for a Nevada ...untry club community.

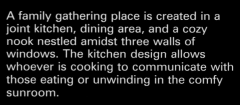

A family gathering place is created in a joint kitchen, dining area, and a cozy nook nestled amidst three walls of windows. The kitchen design allows whoever is cooking to communicate with those eating or unwinding in the comfy sunroom.

An elegant living room opens upward to a balcony on the second floor. It faces an elegant spiral staircase.

34

The master bed and bath enjoy a porch overlooking the private courtyard, a corner whirlpool tub, and a warm fireplace with marble surround.

Antique horses frame the balcony view looking down on the living room. Nearby, a guest room is brightened by sliding doors opening to a spacious second-floor deck.

3. Built for Builders

Built to show off concrete's capabilities, this home was designed to incorporate decorative concrete flatwork, a cement-based stucco finish, and concrete landscaping pavers and retaining walls. What visitors saw, though, when the doors were opened during the International Builders Show in Dallas Texas in 2000, was a luxurious place to live.

Marshall Bobbitt, the developer, gambled on this and three other showcase homes for the event, and found that people are eager to pay for the quality.

"There are a lot of advantages to having a concrete home, advantages that many homeowners are willing to pay a little extra for," he said. "Pest resistance and soundproofing, energy efficiency, and the strength of concrete walls for safety, add to the value of the house."

The house was built using an ICF system by Owens Corning.

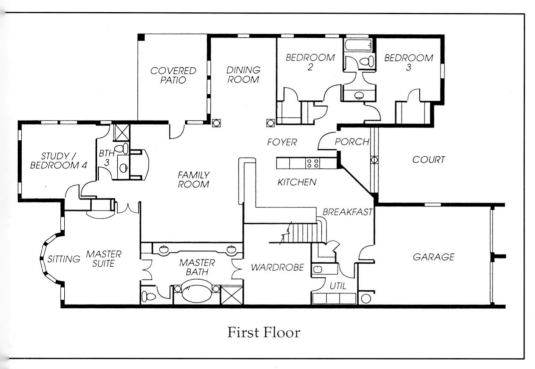

First Floor

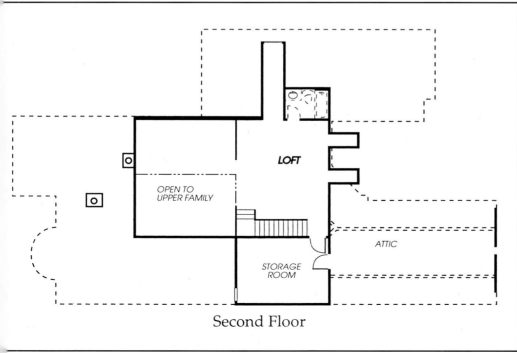

Second Floor

A stained and imprinted concrete walk leads the way to this beautiful showplace home. Built as an example of the design flexibility and beauty possible with concrete construction, this house is now a comfortable home for a family near Dallas, Texas.

cathedral ceiling soars over the wood floors of the family room. Handcrafted millwork outlines the roofline, and creates an elegant fireplace surround.

A gourmet kitchen opens toward a sunny breakfast nook. Nearby, a lavishly appointed dining room rises to a domed ceiling from which hangs an elegant chandelier. Below, custom, footed cabinetry creates a buffet and china cabinet.

The sunny master suite features a semi-circle bay of picture windows, a spacious walk-in closet, and a Mediterranean-themed bathroom complete with ocean-view mural. Lighting under the custom cabinetry emphasizes the footed features of the vanity.

The loft space is used as a private family retreat, within earshot of the home, but secluded and airy. An alleyway leading off toward a window was designed as a practice putting green for a golf enthusiast. Another adjacent room was designed to change, functioning as a children's playroom, an office, or storage space as the homeowner's needs shift.

4. Dream to Sell

The danger in building a dream house lies in one's inability to sell it.

In St. Louis there is an annual event where builders and developers take lots (literally) and then build showcase homes on them. Once completed, these homes are opened to the public for tour, and then sold off.

The custom homebuilding company of HIW, Inc. drew a lot that sloped gently into a wooded area, and engineer/builder Gary W. Schwartz, P.E., designed a rambling ranch with a walkout basement lit by a two-story atrium. Schwartz worked with his concrete suppliers, Breckenridge and River Cement Sales Company, to build a home that showcased concrete's practicality and beauty. Besides being used in the ICF frame

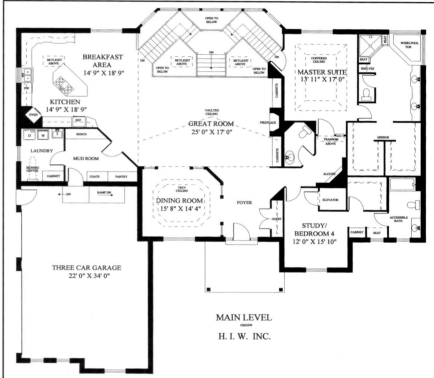

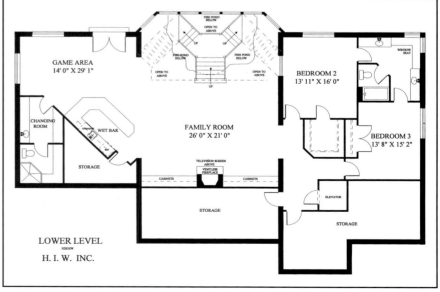

for the home, concrete "cultured stone" was used for exterior accents, as well as for a fireplace surround and the structural concrete pier supporting an atrium stairway. "It's cheaper than real stone, and you can never get enough of the real stone to do a large job that would be consistent. It would cost you a fortune," Schwartz said.

Additionally, a concrete floor in the lower level was tinted and stamped to look like tile, and concrete underlay supports hardwood flooring and carpeting throughout the house to deaden sound. Besides the cultured concrete stone, exterior finishing included fiber cement siding that onlookers swear is wood, but instead is maintenance-free "hardi siding." Even the hearth on the fireplace, a dead-ringer for limestone, was cast of concrete. The same ARXX™ ICF supplied by Breckenridge Material Company were even put to use to encase the vinyl-lined swimming pool, helping to save energy during seasons when the water is heated.

Schwartz lavished beauty elements on his creation – maximizing a two-story wall of windows around his atrium to furnish sunlight to an indoor garden and fishpond, as well as an upstairs great room and a downstairs family room. The atrium houses a floating staircase and overlooks a pool. The view from outside is equally inspired. To add interest and opportunity for artistic embellishment, he added lots of angles to his interior walls, as well as display niches and built-in shelves. Besides creating wow-inspiring views both upstairs, down, and even from outside, Schwartz made his home wheelchair accessible. An elevator in the house has back-up battery power, and all entrances are accessible. In addition, closets were fitted with racks that raise and lower on a hydraulic system, sinks were situated with wheelchair access in mind, light switches set lower. Temperature and light controls were placed bedside, along with a panic button that will flash exterior lights and raise the garage doors for emergency personnel. It's a great house to grow old in.

There were dozens of thoughtful features like this included in the plan for the home. The problem with the house, though, was that the builder and his wife, Monica, couldn't sell it – they wanted it too much themselves. They ended up selling their 120-year-old farmhouse instead and moving in!

Cultured concrete mimics stone, adding interest to the facade of this ranch home. It's humble curb appearance hides an impressive interior.

A heated outdoor pool affords a view inside, to a beautiful suspended staircase in a two-story atrium.

A great room on the main level provides sweeping visual contact between kitchen, dining room, living room, and over an open staircase and two-story view into the backyard. Painted beams over the kitchen define a more intimate area next to the cathedral ceiling.

A pull-down bar by the toilet doubles as a towel rack, and a walk-in shower provides universal access.

5. Master of the House

It's easy to tell who was being spoiled when this home was built – the dog. A spacious indoor kennel serves as entryway for the owner when they pull into their three-car garage. If the dog's not waiting there, it may be that he's out enjoying his private, covered patio.

The owners didn't stint themselves, either. Everyone's needs are accounted for. There's a whole room dedicated to someone's favorite hobby – golf. And a separate study to serve as a significant other's retreat. The volunteer who undertakes the odious chore of bill paying has a nice desk by the fire. The guests may be invited to sit in a beautifully appointed dining room, or to hang out downstairs where an entertainment center and a wet bar create an obvious draw.

This home is rich on leisure space, with 4,008 finished square feet, and another 346 unfinished. It was designed by Vince Kunasek, built by Bruce Schendt.

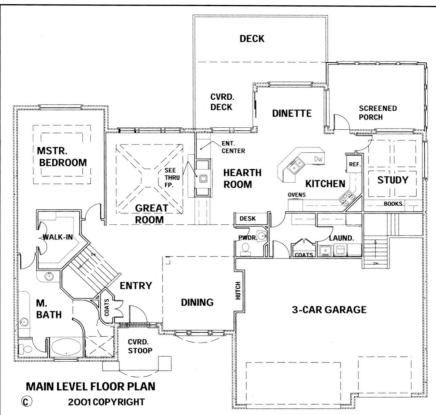

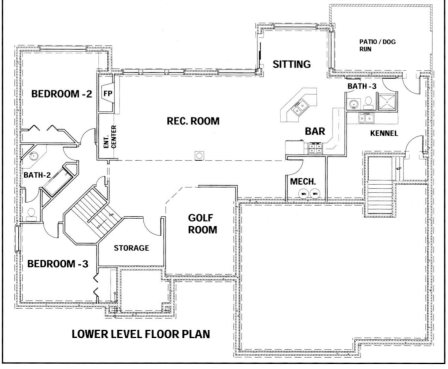

Jeffrey Bebee Photography, Omaha, Nebraska

Jeffrey Bebee Photography, Omaha, Nebraska

The main level of this home sits at street level and opens up in the back with covered deck that in turn shelters patio area below. A covered stoop is part of an impressive entry into a grand foyer.

Jeffrey Bebee Photography, Omaha, Nebraska

58

An intimate seating area on the lower level, in a corner of the recreation room.

Jeffrey Bebee Photography, Omaha, Nebraska

ide the foyer opens into a spacious
iled area where guests are greeted.

The great room encompasses a picture window view, with a
sea-through fireplace into the hearth room by the kitchen.

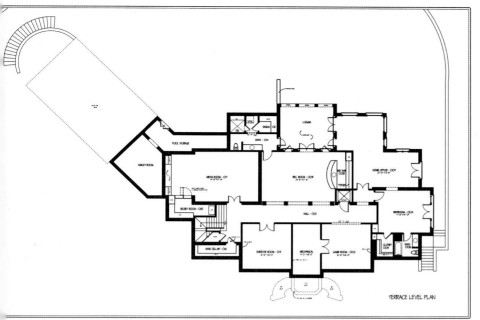

TERRACE LEVEL PLAN

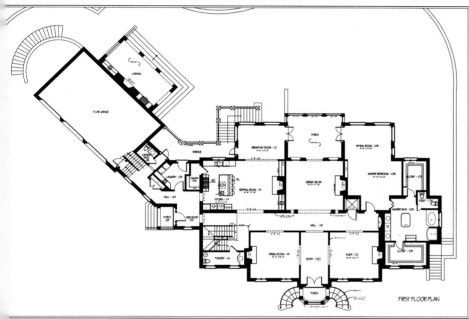

FIRST FLOOR PLAN

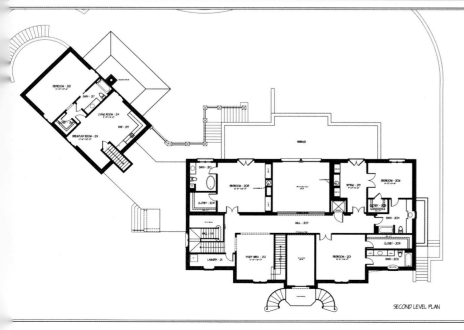

SECOND LEVEL PLAN

6. Amazing Innovations

Harrison Design Associates Principal Bill Harrison likes concrete so much he built his own home out of it. So when he was offered a chance to do a showcase home, he was ready to show off the possibilities to builders.

Harrison, principal of Harrison Design Associates, said that 20 to 25 percent of his residential projects use concrete construction. Concrete, he points out, is "permanent, it's durable. It's much stronger than wood frame. You build your safe room out of concrete, so why not build the whole home that way?" Cost has been one factor in the popularity of wood over concrete, Harrison said, but that's changing. "Wood prices have continued to escalate, and that makes concrete more affordable." More importantly, Harrison feels that homeowner's long-term goals are shifting "as our nation matures. In the 1970s and '80s, people wanted quantity over quality. Today we're seeing more emphasis on quality."

Because this was a showplace home, where the doors would open to attendees of the nation's largest convention, plus the general public, and then go on the market, Harrison designed an everyman home. "It has a typical central entrance and formal entertainment areas up front, with the casual living areas along the back, opening to the backyard and swimming pool," he said.

Named the "Manufacturer's Dream Home 2000," it would be anyone's dream home. In all, it has over 13,573 square feet of heated/air-conditioned space including a finished attic, plus a garage, garage apartment, and grill area.

It sold almost immediately!

61

Opposite page: This eclectic French manor looks as thou
it's been standing for centuries, yet it was built using
latest foam form concrete wall technology, as well as us
decorative concrete pavers to outline and define
entryway. *Courtesy of Harrison Design Associa*

The home's furnishings define opulence while reserving comfort. Overstuffed is key to all the seating. Warm gold and honey brown tones unify the home and create a comforting ambience. *Courtesy of Harrison Design Associates*

Deborah Whitlaw Photographer

Deborah Whitlaw Photographer

Deborah Whitlaw Photographer

Layers of molding add architectural detail and are key to
the illusion that this home has been occupied for centuries. *Courtesy of Harrison Design Associates*

Boutchine Photography

Elegantly appointed kitchen and master bath
include custom cabinetry and granite countertops.
Courtesy of Harrison Design Associates

7. Architect's Own

Atlanta, Georgia's Bill Harrison, an AIA Associate, has designed more than 3,000 homes, and none received so much thought as his own. Harrison and his wife, Deborah, called on two philosophies when building their own home – they wanted the house to look as though it had been in the family for hundreds of years, and they wanted it to last for hundreds of years after they built it. So they built using cast concrete and reinforced concrete block walls.

"It's permanent, it's durable – much stronger than wood frame," says Harrison. "When people think of concrete, they think of modern, contemporary, stark. Yet the Romans used concrete. It's not a new product. In fact, most of Italy is concrete."

An enthusiastic student of architectural history, Harrison designed a home for himself in Palladian Villa style, adding Tuscan influences. He and his wife found recycled flooring, chestnut beams from an old barn in Pennsylvania, and antique terracotta tile from Europe to soften their home and add elegance and age. It has the feel of villas from the 14th and 15th century, Harrison said.

"Concrete is just good for the bones. Like drinking your milk when you're a kid. You want good strong bones in your house," Harrison said. After that, you want to accessorize.

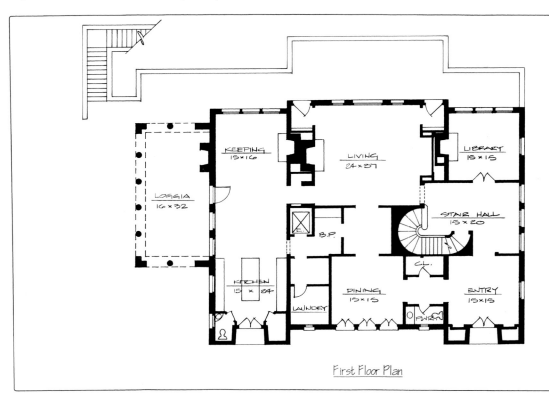

First Floor Plan

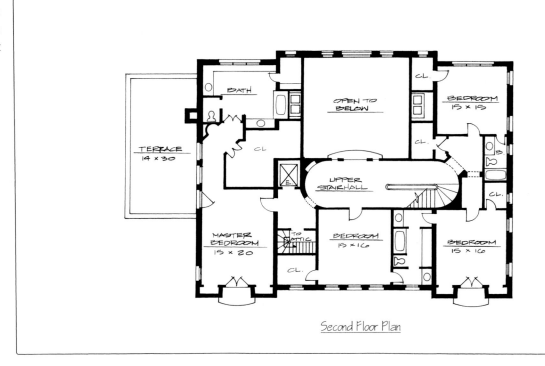

Second Floor Plan

Mural wallpaper sandwiched between drapes of foliage hue create a
wooded room for indoor picnics. A chandelier adds elegance and
romance. *Courtesy of Harrison Design Associates*

Boutchine Photography

cco finish caps this classic example of Palladian architecture, marked by
fectly symmetrical features, including double front entrances with stone-capped
hed portals topped by wrought-iron encased balconies. *Courtesy of Harrison
sign Associates*

73

Photo by Lynn McGill

Photo by Lynn McGill

Arched windows echo throughout the house, harking back to the designer's mentor, Andrea Palladio, an Italian who designed concrete homes centuries ago. *Courtesy of Harrison Design Associates*

Photo by Lynn McGill

Imported antique tiles in kitchen and "keeping" area help create the impression that this home has been part of the family for eons.
Courtesy of Harrison Design Associates

An advantage of the Atlanta climate is temperate weather that allows these homeowners to enjoy an outdoor room throughout much of the year. A fireplace helps take the chill out of spring and fall evenings. *Courtesy of Harrison Design Associates*

An antique wrought iron bed and luxuriant textiles help recreate Italian holidays for these homeowners. *Courtesy of Harrison Design Associates*

Photo by Lynn McGill

fireplace is always a room's focal point. Here two wonderful very different reatments create vastly different rooms. Around one, an antique white narble surround creates classic formality. In the other, a simple marble urround is capped by a dramatic painting and newspaper-ed wall for a nore intimate setting. *Courtesy of Harrison Design Associates*

by Lynn McGill

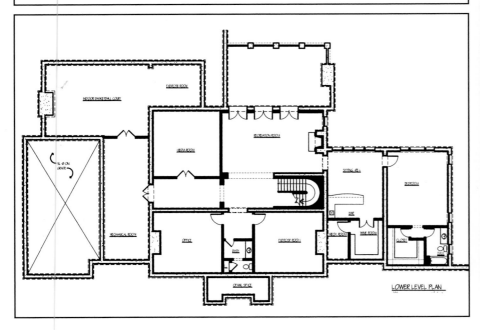

MAIN LEVEL PLAN

SECOND LEVEL PLAN

LOWER LEVEL PLAN

8. Safe Haven

For an Atlanta show home, an impressive array of builders, manufacturers, and
designers came together to design a home
that incorporated a "safe room." This concrete room has been named the best way

Photography ©William P. Steele

to reduce the loss of life and minimize personal injury from the ravages of tornadoes and hurricanes, according to the Federal Emergency Management Agency (FEMA). Besides a concrete safe room, which doubles as a walk-in closet, the house incorporates the most innovative home controls and security systems. Further, the outside walls were all constructed using ICF walls to guarantee the safest structure possible.

Designed by Atlanta architectural designer William Harrison, the 6,000-plus square foot home was built by Benecki Fine Homes. Inside, a luxurious sense of scale and an open floor plan

provides a large public area with 14-foot ceilings and various ceiling treatments to create monumental architecture. Designed in French-country style, the home reflects the needs and concerns of a busy family. A dual home office is wired for a computer and fitted with a large fireplace for warmth and comfort. With close proximity to the front entrance, the location of the office is perfect for work-at-home or bringing-work-home parents.

The home was open for tours during the National Association of Home Builders show in Atlanta in 2001, and sold immediately afterward. The new owners enjoy a home that is both beautiful, and ready to stand up to the best tests of time and nature.

Petal yellow and white brighten a spacious kitchen

Although not a room that highlights a tour of this spacious home, the safe room is truly at the heart of its design. Serving as a wonderful walk-in closet, this is also where the owners store their valuables, and where the family would flee in the event of a storm or other emergency that required four strong walls for safety.

The Safe Haven home incorporates a number of gathering areas for family and friends. A wealth of fireplaces turn each into an intimate place, and a bright yellow on the walls adds cheer.

Upstairs bedrooms incorporate private baths, recessed windows, and the poetry of slanting eaves.

9. Country Style

Fire safety, weather resistance, and beautiful design were all wrapped into one for this Houston area show house, in a plan by Home Design Services that demonstrates concrete's best benefits. The exterior of this concrete block home was finished with a concrete stucco coating and stone "cultured" from concrete to be a dead ringer for Texas limestone. Cultured stone offers quality control in the manufacturing process, durability, and low maintenance. The roof is also concrete – with concrete roof tiles to lend an air of elegance, and another protective barrier against termites, fire, and weather.

Other concrete elements were incorporated into this show home, built by G.A. Bumpass Builders, Inc., including decorative concrete floors in the kitchen and dining areas, and pattern-stamped and colored concrete paving in the porches and driveway.

Home Design Services, Inc.

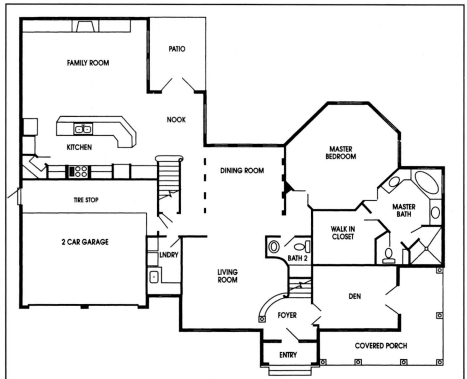

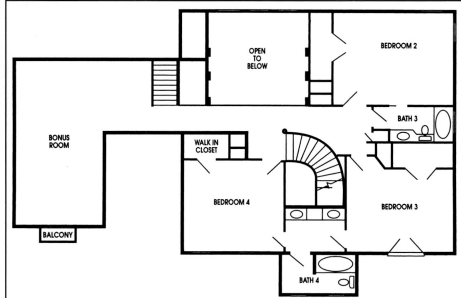

You don't know it looking at this home, but what you're seeing is an ultra-strong concrete building, finished in cultured concrete stone, concrete stucco, and capped by concrete roof tiles. The package is a sure-fire deterrent to everything from hurricane force winds to ghetto-blaster car sound systems.

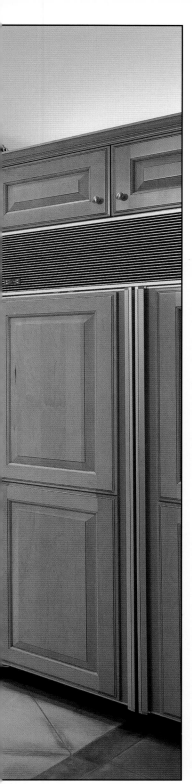

A decorative concrete floor adds warmth and character to this spacious kitchen. The color variations were achieved used hand-cast coloring powders that actually create a harder, more durable concrete surface. The floor is carried through into the family room, where a fireplace is the focal point under a vaulted ceiling.

©Rob Muir

Designers from the Texas Gulf Coast Chapter of the American Society of Interior Designers went wild with color in this living room, making a daring and delightful statement with hot pink and lemon tones against olive drab walls.

A faux storm threatens imaginary laundry in this creatively appointed laundry room.

©Rob Muir

96

A stately den opens out to a covered porch, where cultured stone
and classic pillars create an ageless ambience.

Muir

This 3,915-square-foot home includes three bedrooms upstairs, as well as two nicely appointed baths.

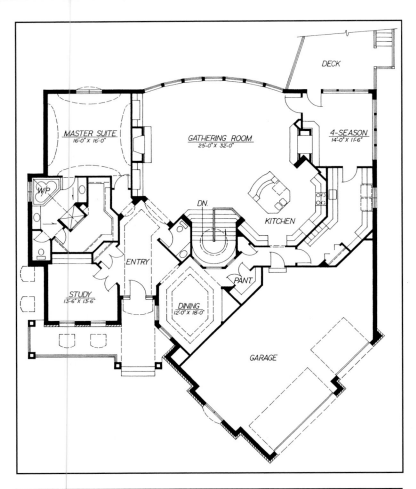

10. Street of Dreams

In Nebraska, they have a show called the Omaha Street of Dreams where builders and designers team up to build spec houses for public tour and sale. This one was named best of show in 1998, and understandably so. Besides a design that eschews square-box rooms, this 5,169 square foot home was built with insulating concrete forms and declared the "most energy efficient and most structurally sound of any home ever displayed in Omaha."

People have been lining up for ICF constructed homes ever since.

The builder is a big advocate. Curt Hofer built his own home using ICF construction.

This is a home designed for a family that plays together, with great gathering spaces including a fantastic great room with a semi-circular bay of windows attached kitchen, and an enormous fireplace decorated with the same cultured concrete "river stone" found on the exterior of the house. There is also a four-season room, as well as a recreational room, wet bar, game area, and exercise room for this busy family.

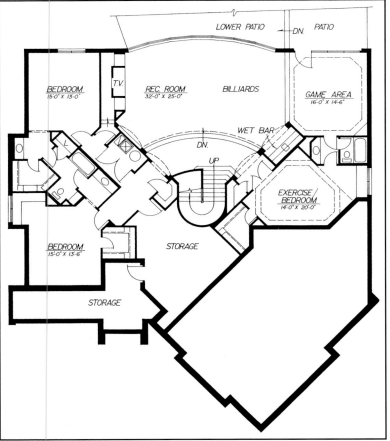

Opposite page: The entry/foyer area is typ of this home in that the walls do not proc along straight, predictable lines. Instead, entry flares open leading to various areas of home. *Courtesy of Curt Hofer Construction,*

Courtesy of Curt Hofer Construction, I

Jeffrey Bebee Photographer

Jeffrey Bebee Photographer

The kitchen and living area open to a wonderful view out a bow of solid glass. *Courtesy of Curt Hofer Construction, Inc.*

A richly furnished study enjoys a soaring ceiling with transom-like windows to allow in light. *Courtesy of Curt Hofer Construction, Inc.*

To highlight the versatility of co
crete, three houses were built for tou
during the 1997 National Associatio
of Home Builders Show in Bellair
Texas. Two fathers and sons, two ge
erations of architects, two of builde
were teamed up to create an IC
showplace.

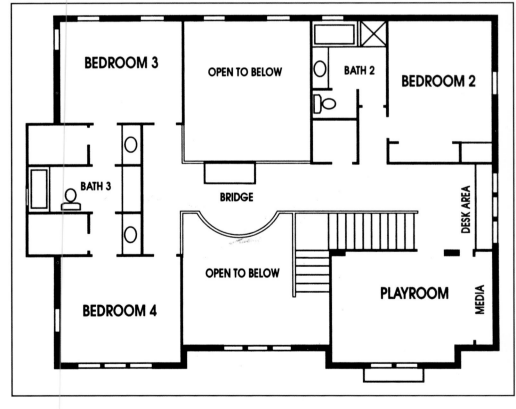

A stone exterior is actually "cultured" of concrete for a realistic, strong, practical, and affordable application to add glamour and value to a home.

It was Jeffrey Berkus who worked with his father, Barry, to design a modified Prairie-style home, which was then built by Andy and Martin Perlman of A. Lexis Homes, Inc. "It was a very cool house," Jeffrey Berkus said. "We were able to use the ICF in very creative ways to get a very custom looking house. We sited the house around existing trees. I really advocate the "green home" concept, of environmental responsibility, and concrete construction helps achieve this goal. We love concrete." I've used it in floors, countertops, pretty much anywhere you can imagine."

The home design suits a family with parents who plan to stay awhile. The master bedroom is on the main floor, to facilitate universal access. Upstairs there are three bedrooms and a playroom with plenty of space for homework or a media center. A bonus room over the garage

©Rob Muir

108

is perfect for a nanny or a hobby room. An exercise room overlooks a private terrace.

Father and son Andy and Martin Perlman of A. Lexis Home, Inc. worked with the Berkus team to build the house.

Concrete countertops were textured and colored for an attractive yet durable surface. "I like the material better than granite or tile because it gives it a feeling of age, time, and durability," says architect Jeffrey Berkus.

A balcony commands a view of a two-story reception area in the home. An open fireplace warms both the entry area and a living room beyond.

The living room commands a view of the private terrace.

Here's where the work gets done: while the laundry's spinning, the wheels are doing the same on an exercise bike next door.

Muir

The four bedrooms of this show house were lavishly appointed by members of the Texas Gulf Coast Chapter of the American Society of Interior Decorators.

12. Casa del Mar

A block from the Atlantic, this model home was built to introduce potential residents to a new 2,200-acre community in Myrtle Beach. This house had to be attractive to customers ready to buy in an oceanfront community complete with beach club, championship golf course, tennis and fitness facilities.

"After months of researching exterior wall systems, we found that ICFs had the most to offer, with surprisingly little cost difference compared to conventional framing methods," said Philip Troutman, vice president of construction for Seacoast Communities, Inc. "Being close to the ocean made ICF's superior wind resistance very attractive. Its unequaled R-value, sound protection, reduced air infiltration, and termite and moisture resistance gives us confidence we are offering our homeowners a product consistent with the lifestyle they have chosen."

The concrete forms were erected in an Italianate design by Kevin J. Smudde Designs. Sally Stowe Interiors, Inc. was brought on board to furnish the home in a manor befitting the Italianate architecture. The end result, as you see here, is a lavish home fit for the best of company.

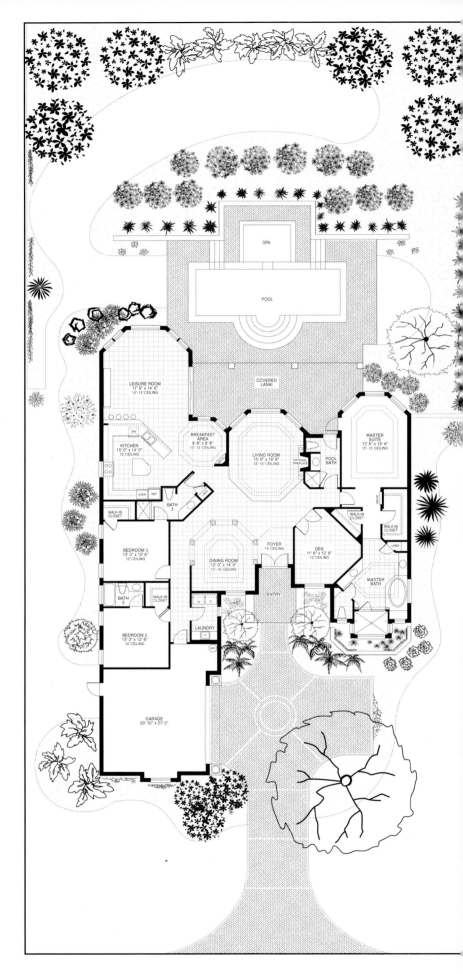

Sunlight illuminates the family's "leisure room," featuring a built-in entertainment unit.

An octagonal living room with drop ceiling is furnished in velvets and damask for rich effect.

Palm trees, cement stucco siding, and a concrete tile roof add up to a tropical paradise. This model home showcases the best in coastal living.

Comfort wasn't sacrificed when this intimate dining room was furnished for formal entertaining.

Bright cabinetry and granite countertops characterize this kitchen. The refrigerator is concealed behind panels made to match.

The lavish furnishings didn't stop at the door to the master bath and bedroom.

13. Grand Entry

This enormous, 5,200 square foot ranch makes a huge impression on first entry. It was meant to. It was built to demonstrate energy efficient, durable construction for Omaha's Showcase of Better Built Homes. Guests to the fifteen-room home are stunned by the first view on entering a barrel vault entryway. The tiled foyer opens out to an enormous great room with amazing views.

Design Basics worked creative configurations into the basic form of the home, to add interest to room shapes. The home was packed with pretty features including, oak doors, jams and casings inside with brass hardware, brass plumbing fixtures, and a long list of little extras. Furthermore, it was presented and sold fully furnished, decorated by Mary Ehly of Ehly's Decorating, Inc.

A finished basement designed by builder Jerry Kessler includes amenities like a full bath, entertainment, guest, and bonus rooms.

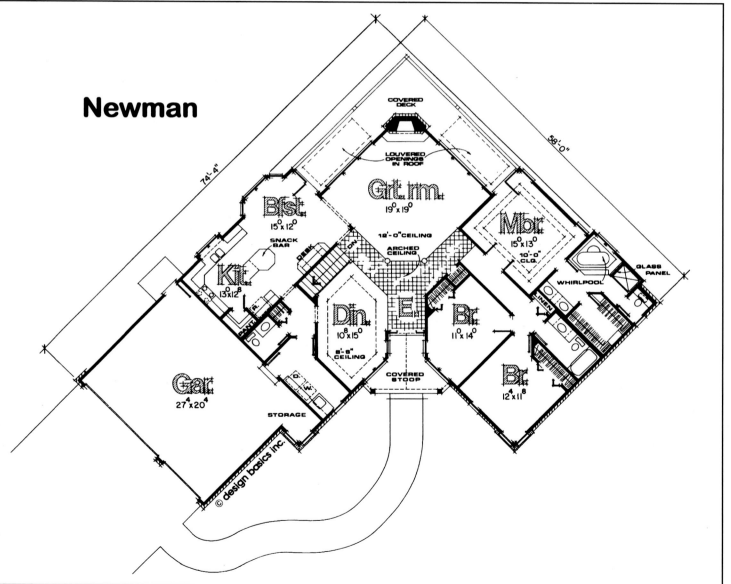

Newman

Jeffrey Bebee Photographer, Omaha

A covered porch and brick fascia are a prelude to an eye-popping entrance to this spacious ranch.

A barrel-vaulted entry opens to an impressive great room beyond.

A red accent stripe draws the eye up to fancy molding work in the master bedroom.

Above and opposite page bottom: The
finished basement includes a gas fireplace/
entertainment center and was furnished with a
gaming table.

Jeffrey Bebee Photographer, Omaha

The great room and a dinette open to a railed deck and an attractive woodland view.

14. Case Dolce

A lush center courtyard overlooked by a rooftop garden. It's Mediterranean living in the Northwest. The house was built for the Street of Dreams event in Portland, Oregon, where builders and designers team up to build spec houses for public tour and sale. This house stole a

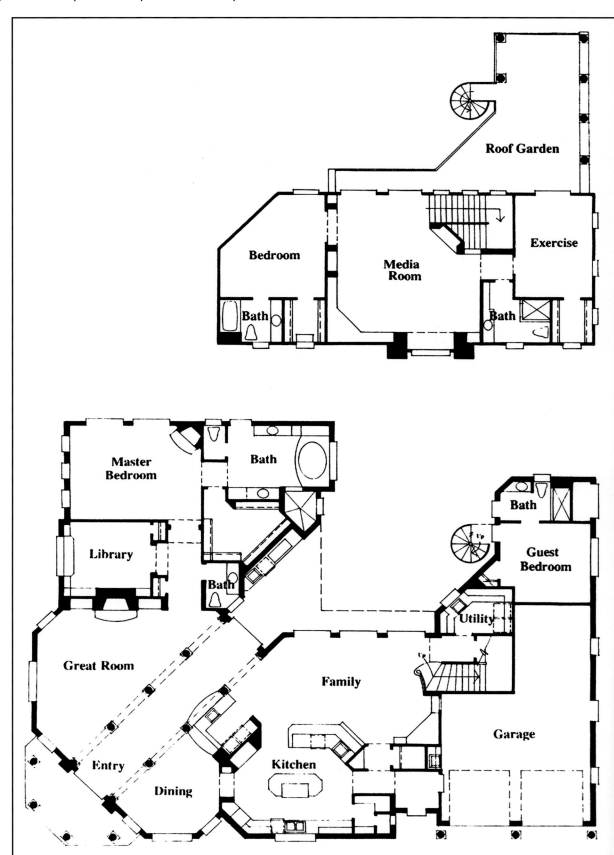

Stucco exterior finish, and arched portals and windows under a red tiled roof create the impression of a Mediterranean retreat for this Omaha-area home.

At the heart of this home is a wonderful outdoor room. The private courtyard is complete with a soothing waterfall, barbeque, and a wet bar. A rooftop garden overlooks all.

lot of hearts. Designers at Olson Group Architects, AIA, had a very active couple in mind when they designed this home. The house is a dream home for people who love to entertain. Aside from the master bedroom, the architects incorporated two very private and remote guest rooms with separate baths and entrances. There are multiple rooms for both casual and formal entertaining, including a media room. And a wet bar is located in the very center of the home.

The 4,640 square foot home has a casual, intimate feel, underlined with a radiant heat system in the floors. The luxury project was outlined in ICF walls built by Blazer Development, Inc. and Ash Grove Cement Company. The house also incorporates a state-of-the-art lighting control system, which gives the owner convenient, single-button controllable lighting zones throughout the house.

A rich wood finish mutes the stainless steel efficiency of a modern kitchen.

A family room off the kitchen area allows the family to congregate before or after the meal. An adjacent wet bar is in the center of the home, for a family that loves to entertain.

The dining areas and the great room are on either side of the entryway.

A wonderful coffee table is padded for extra seating and, miraculously, the table stands up to reveal the controls for a surround sound media center.

Built-in shelves line a reader's retreat, a warm
library dedicated to literature.

Master bed and bath, like the rest of the home, enjoy huge arched windows for a flood of warm light.

15. Symphony Show House

Here's what happens when a whole host of creative people team up to create a home. This project benefited Florida's Jacksonville Symphony Association, and was designed by Kevin Gray Residential Designs and finished by the North Florida chapter of the American Society of Interior Design. The results are stunning.

From grand entertaining to intimate family affairs, the 7,300-square-foot, 2.6 million French Mediterranean-style home reveals a thoughtful understanding of today's lifestyle. In addition to every luxury you could imagine in a residence of this magnitude, Collier Classic Homes builders utilized the most innovative building products on the market today, including ICF walls installed by Force One.

The home helped to introduce ICF wall construction. The tour's big, glossy booklet described ICF as the fastest method of constructing a fully insulated concrete wall, price competitive, excellent for areas subject to hurricane-force winds, impervious to structural damage from wood eating termites and carpenter ants, and super energy efficient, higher appraisal values, lower insurance rates, reduced airborne pollution and dust allergens, and an end to noise pollution.

Hundreds of people lined up to tour the home during three weeks of open house events, their admission fees helping to develop music programs for Jacksonville-area schools.

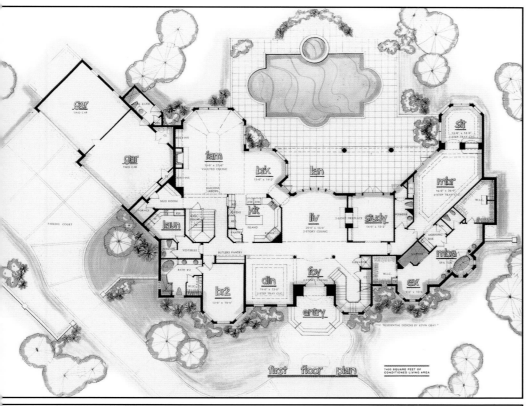

Collier Classic Homes
of Ponte Vedra

Elegant curb appeal opens up to resort-style living in the back, focused around patio and pool.

Family is the focus of the home's biggest room, where an intimate portrait enjoys center stage on a massive fireplace surround, set beneath a vaulted ceiling.

A see-through fireplace creates a connection between the living room and this paneled study.

Neo-classical detailing adds elegant flair to this old-world kitchen.

Layering and details create luxury in the expansive master bed and adjacent sitting area and bath.

Resource Guide

ARXX Building Products
840 Division Street
Cobourg Ontario K9A5V2 Canada
1-800-293-3210
www.arxxbuild.com

A&S Steel Framing, Inc.
1461 Highway 98 West
Mary Esther, FL 32569
850-978-2343
www.arxxbuild.com

A. Lexis Home, Inc.
5090 Richmond Ave., Ste. 105
Houston, TX 77056
713-871-1116

American Society of Interior Decorators
608 Massachusetts Ave. N.E.
Washington, DC 20002
202-546-3480

Ash Grove Cement Company
6720 SW Macadam Ave. Ste. 300
Portland, OR 97219
503-293-2333

Benecki Fine Homes
11 Putnam Dr. NW
Atlanta, GA 30342
404-760-8900

Berkus Design Studio
2020 A.P.S., Suite 133
Santa Barbara, CA 93103
805-963-8901
www.berkusdesignstudio.com
www.b3architects.com

Blazer Development
PO Box 1410
Lake Oswego, Oregon 97034
503-598-3992
www.blazerdevelopment.com

Bost Construction Company
219 East Chatham St., Ste. 205
Cary, NC 27511
919-460-1983

Breckenridge Material Company
2833 Breckenridge Industrial Court
St. Louis, M 63144
314-962-1234

Brock and Weigle Construction, Inc.
3570 Barron Way, Suite D
Reno, NV 89511
775-827-8668

Bruce Schendt, Structures and Concrete
  Paving
Box 24489
Omaha, NE 68124
402-672-2502

Clifford Taylor Architects PC
219 West Colorado Avenue #300
Colorado Springs, CO 80903
719-633-4592
www.staia.com

Collier Classic Homes, Inc.
217 Ponte Vedra Park Dr. Ste. 400
Ponte Vedra Beach, FL 32082
904-273-6776
www.collierclassichomes.com

Curt Hofer Construction, Inc.
2332 Bob Boozer Drive
Omaha, NE 68130
402-758-0440
www.curthofer.com

Design Basics, Inc.
11112 John Galt Blvd.
Omaha, NE 68137
402-331-9223
www.designbasics.com

Ed Zweigle Enterprises
PO Box 8248
Truckee, CA 96162
530-587-8656
www.edzweigle-ent.com

Ehly's Decorating, Inc.
2312 Bob Boozer Drive
Omaha, NE 68130
402-330-6557

EPS Building Systems L.L.C.
Box 1018
Brighton, CO 80601
303-655-8205
www.epswall.com

Essroc Cement Co.
3251 Bath Pike
Nazareth, PA 18064
610-837-6725
www.essroc.com

Force One Walls
10450 US 1 North Ste. 1
St. Augustine, FL 32095
904-285-1005

Fred Wynn, AIA
Dallas Design Group Architects
9330 LBJ Suite 1010
Dallas, TX 75243
972-907-0080
www.fredwynnarchitect.com

G.A. Bumpass Builders, Inc.
9 Alabama Court
Houston, TX 77027
713-626-4626

Harrison Design Associates
3198 Cains Hill Place, NW Ste. 200
Atlanta, GA 30305
404-365-7760
www.harrisondesignassociates.com

HIW Inc.
6731 Manchester Road
St. Louis, MO 63139
314-644-2111
www.stlouiscustombuilder.com

Home Design Services
580 Cape Cod Lane, Suite 9
Altamonte Springs, FL 32714
800-771-5444

Jeffrey Berkus Architects
1100 West Sixth, Suite D
Austin, TX 78703
512-478-5259

Kessler Custom Builders, Inc.
912 Killarney Drive
Papillion, NE 68406
402-339-1180

Kevin Gray Residential Designs
1478 S. Third St.
Jacksonville Beach, FL 32250
904-246-0058
www.kevingray.com

Kevin J. Smudde Designs
8800 University Pkwy, Suite B2
Pensacola, FL 32514
850-478-2842

Lake Crest Homes
775-846-9690

Marshall Bobbitt Homes
2 Bright Meadows
Heath, TX 75032
214-912-6487

Olson Group Architects, AIA
17150 SW Upper Boones Ferry Road
Durham, OR 97224
503-620-9870

O'Shea Builders
PO Box 5709
Destin, FL 32540
1-850-654-8600

Precision Concrete Construction, Inc.
5955 Shiloh Road E., Ste. 200
Alpharetta, GA 30005
770-751-3887

Reward Wall Systems
4115 S 87th Street
Omaha, NE 68127
800-468-6344
www.rewardwalls.com

Richie and Associates Architects
1100 Caughlin Crossing
Reno, NV 89509

River Cement Sales Company
17107 Chesterfield Airport Rd., Ste. 130
Chesterfield, MO 63005
636-532-1060

RiverStone Design/Build
15664 Thirteen Mile Road
RR#4 Denfield
Ontario NOM 1PO Canada
519-461-0166
www.concretehouses.com

Sally Stowe Interiors, Inc.
7823 North Kings Hwy.
Myrtle Beach, SC 29572
843-692-2603

Seacoast Communities, Inc.
1507 Trade Street
Myrtle Beach, SC 29577
843-626-7493

Sterling Penman
Box 202
Green Mountain, CO 80819
719-684-9562

Vince Kunasek Design, Inc.
13913 Greenfield Road
Omaha, NE 68138
402-896-2421